ANNI & CARSTEN SENNOV

I0540513

ENERGY
SELF-DEFENSE
for
MEN

good adventures publishing

Energy Self-Defense for Men

©2017, Anni & Carsten Sennov and Good Adventures Publishing
First edition, first impression
Set with Cambria
Layout: Anni Sennov – www.sennovpartners.com
Cover design: Michael Bernth – www.monovoce.dk
Author photo: Aamod & Sophelia Korhonen - www.balanceisjoy.com

ISBN 978-87-7206-001-9

Contents

Notice

When reading this book please be in a spirit of open-mindedness.

Although the authors and the publisher have made every effort to ensure the accuracy and completeness of information contained in this book, we assume no responsibility for errors, inaccuracies, omissions, or any inconsistencies herein. Any offense caused to people, places, or organizations is unintentional.

Readers should use their own judgment, or consult a holistic medical expert or their personal physician for specific applications to their individual problems.

Welcome

Dear Sir!

We hereby welcome you to benefit from this helpful energy guide called *"Energy Self-Defense for Men"*. In this book, we focus on supporting you in your effort to live a successful and balanced life by giving you Energy Self-Defense tools that you can use in all relationships and situations, both at work and in your personal life.

This Energy Self-Defense guide is for **all** men no matter your age, background, social status, or personality.

You will learn how to take care of your personal energy in daily situations, and how and when to use specific Energy Self-Defense tools so you never lose energy again. We will even teach you how to bring back all the energy that you have already lost.

From our experience, we know that most men prefer things to be tangible and logical. Learning about the invisible energy we all carry with us will be new and very useful. The Energy Self-Defense tools in this book will work for you even if you have never worked with energy on a conscious level before. We challenge you to give it a try and be positively surprised.

Enjoy reading!

Anni & Carsten Sennov

What is Energy Self-Defense and how to get started

Energy Self-Defense is about learning how to look after your own energy, so you don't lose energy throughout your day. The more personal energy you lose, the harder it is to achieve the things you dream about doing.

Energy Self-Defense tools can even be used to take back the part of your personal energy that you lost a long time ago – and who wouldn't like to get all their personal energy and power back home where it belongs?

At first, the Energy Self-Defense tools in this book will be an extra detail to add to your to-do list. It will require a bit of practice to remember these techniques on a daily basis. The good news is, that after a short time, these exercises will eventually only take a few minutes of your time to do each day, and can be done anywhere; even when you are around other people, and without anyone even noticing what you are doing.

There are many Energy Self-Defense tools that can be used to convert negative energy into positive, and the Energy Self-Defense tools described in this book work very well for most men, so just give it a try and see what happens.

That said, we do recommend that you ask for divine protection before you start working with any kind of Energy Self-Defense exercises. This can also be used when you feel a little exposed and want to protect yourself.

Simply recite this protection prayer out loud or quietly to yourself:

"I pray for Divine protection
from the highest Divine Source."

If you haven't worked with Energy Self-Defense exercises before, we recommend that you sit in a quiet place the first few times you do it. Sit with your eyes closed, take some deep breaths, and relax before you get started, since it can be difficult to concentrate if there are a lot of disturbances around you.

After a while you will be able to use the Energy Self-Defense tools and do the exercises you will learn in this book everywhere you go, and no one else will know what's going on. Suddenly sorting and balancing your energy on a daily basis will become second nature for you.

What is Energy Exchange?

What is energy exchange, and why it is important to know about this.

We all use energy terms like:

- I'm full of energy
- He has a negative attitude and energy
- What a strong energy, charisma and radiance she has

These are terms that most people are familiar with, and you have probably experienced how it feels to be attracted and/ or repelled to certain people and the energy they radiate. You might have even felt the energy exchange that exists between two people in love, where you can often see and sense the sparks in the air between them.

Most of us have also felt exhausted after certain work meetings, and conversely, felt full of energy after spending time with great friends.

Energy exchange is when two or more people are together, and they consciously or subconsciously impact each other. Most of the time this happens at an unconscious level without people even knowing. We have written this series of Energy Self-Defense guides to provide awareness of what happens on the invisible level when being around others. Please feel free to share this information with those you know in order to create a better atmosphere in your personal network.

Protecting yourself from negative energy doesn't mean that you should stay away from other people. You probably get together with other people a lot; therefore you just need to know how to stay balanced and take care of your own energy, which can be done by using the Energy Self-Defense tools in this book.

The 3 ways of exchanging energy

Fundamentally there are three ways in which energy exchange can happen between people, and it's important that you are conscious about this, so you know which exchange is occurring when you are with others.

Here are the 3 ways of exchanging energy:

1) The energy goes both ways

The exchange of energy between two people is happening in a balanced and equal way, creating a positive situation for both of them.

You may be in perfect balance in your relationships with some people, because you support and help each other equally and want to do good things for each other, thus keeping both of you happy

2) The energy only goes one way, but voluntarily

One person is voluntarily sharing parts of their energy, while the other person is receiving the energy.

In this case, you might voluntarily choose to help others just because you want to do something nice for them, and because it makes you happy to do it. They may not have the energy to help you in return or to give you anything back at that moment, but you feel great because they are people that you like and they are happy that you are helping them.

3) The energy only goes one way, but involuntarily

One person is taking energy from another person without this person being conscious about it, resulting in one feeling weaker and drained from energy and the other person, who has gained energy, feeling stronger than before.

And finally, there are the energy thieves – people who want something from you, and who are unhappy no matter how much you help them or give them. In fact, spending time with them and trying to help them will put you in a bad mood and often they will even take energy from you without permission; then you will be in an extremely bad mood.

Raise your energy through relaxation and happiness

There are many ways to raise your energy level. We are sure you already do many of these and feel great afterwards.

Always take time to do the things that raise your energy level, even if you are traveling and staying in a hotel, attending a conference, or being together with those you love.

Sit down and relax in a nice place or in your favorite chair, and listen to your favorite music, read a book (even if you only have time to read a few pages), do a crossword puzzle, or something else that makes your brain relax and feel good at the same time. You can also meditate and do physical exercises that load your body and mind with endorphins.

Go for a walk in nature or in your neighborhood, and do it at your own pace. Take your time to talk with family and friends on the phone as often as you can, even if you don't think you have the time. That will make you happy and raise your personal energy level.

Eat your favorite meal or snack. Do it with good conscience, if it makes you happy. The most important part of doing this is to feel the pleasure and enjoyment when eating your favorite food. If your weight goes up, then go for a run or a long walk, so you can better balance your physical weight, while still enjoying the foods you love. It's important to do the type of exercises and move your body in a way that makes you feel happy and motivated.

Go to the gym, jump up and down, or move around behind your desk at work to make your body feel happy. You can also have sex to feel happy and alive. As long as those you involve also feel happy, you are on the right path. Never try to convince others to do what you want them to do, if they are not happy about doing it. Then you are about to spread negative energy, which is the exact opposite of spreading positive energy and raising your energy level.

Selfish people might be able to convince their brain that everything is okay in their life, even if those around them are not happy. However they can never convince their whole body to be happy if those around them are not happy. This is the reason why most egoistic and selfish people are more likely to be unhappy and cruel to others: because they are actually not happy inside themselves.

You seldom meet happy people who are cruel to others!

Laughing and having fun are also very good and easy ways to raise the energy level in your body and mind.

Here is a list of ways to raise your energy and make you feel happy and motivated:

- *Relax in a nice place*
- *Listen to your favorite music*
- *Read a book, do a crossword puzzle, or something else that makes your brain relax*
- *Meditate*
- *Do physical exercises or go to the gym*
- *Play your favorite sport with friends*
- *Go for a walk*
- *Dance, jump or move around*
- *Talk/meet with people that make you happy*

- *Feel the pleasure and joy when eating your favorite food or snack*
- *Do something that makes you laugh and have fun*
- *Make every day good by doing something extra-ordinary for yourself*

How to be successful at work and in sports

Being successful at work and when playing sports requires some skills, knowledge and experience. So if you have the skills but lack the energy and radiance to attract the right job, you can be sure your situation will change in a positive way by using the Energy Self-Defense tools mentioned in this book. However, the Energy Self-Defense tools cannot help you to be skillful. In that case you will instead need training and education.

Since there are usually many skilled people standing in a line to get a job, it's important to be attractive in more ways beyond simply being qualified for the job. Your radiance and being positive mean a lot, and these qualities are in fact of much greater value in many places than having the right skills and resume experience. Looking good is attractive in itself, but if a good looking person doesn't shine or smile, their good looks are worth almost nothing.

A person's radiance can be sensed thousands of miles away, while a good look can only be seen in-person or in photos. Your radiance emits an energy that is seen by others and is of great importance in all aspects of life.

If you want to have success at work and when playing sports, be professional and always use your skills in a constructive and positive way. Other people will notice you, and if you add a charming personality to your specific skill set, then you will have even greater success in all aspects of life. Of course, none of this works if it is superficial, it must be a genuine part of you, as conversely, others will just as easily sense your insincerity if you contrive a smile or turn on a fake charm.

The following rules and Energy Self-Defense exercises are useful in all situations, and they are especially useful prior to a job interview, sporting event, or when dealing with those who are not closely related to you:

Rule number 1:

Always keep your own energy at home in your own body and personal energy field, where it benefits you and those you think of and care about.

Pull all your rightful energy back to yourself from others in a cleansed form, and send the energy of others out of your energy field and return it to them.

Rule number 2:

Surround yourself with white cleansing light/energy that will make you radiate honesty and positive thinking.

Embrace yourself in white light/energy to dissolve all negativity around you.

Rule number 3:

Surround yourself with love energy that will make people love you more.

Embrace yourself in pink love energy to radiate love all around you.

Rule number 4:

Feel supported by the Divine Source and believe that there is a reason for everything that happens in your life.

Let God be your eternal Divine Source, so everything you want comes to you very quickly, perfectly and in grace.

Try these energy tools out more than once – not just for one day. Give them a chance to take hold and become habitual by using them every day for a week or more. Let them be a part of your daily ritual – just like combing your hair and brushing your teeth. Suddenly you will find that they become a natural part of your personality that will automatically radiate positive energy everywhere you go and in everything you do. By doing this you can't help but be successful at work and in the sports arena, if that is what you want.

If you don't feel like doing all four exercises, then do the ones that you feel the most attracted to whenever you need a certain type of protection or cleaning.

How to be successful at home

If you sometimes feel that your house is more of a battle-field than a loving home, then it's time to look at your own role at home. This is not because you should step more into character, but maybe you should instead be active in creating a positive energy in the house.

In homes where both men and women work on a daily basis, the household and the good atmosphere at home is usually both parties' responsibility, where the tasks have been split up in mutual agreement. However, if the man leaves the house early in the morning to go to work and has long working hours, and the house is his wife's domain, then it's obviously her energy that influences the overall atmosphere at home.

If you are not very much involved at home and you don't know how your children are doing, or notice when your wife has had a haircut, then it's time for you to take action. The Energy Self-Defense tools we recommend cannot do all the work for you, but they can certainly help change your personal radiance and attitude in a positive direction. Then your surroundings – in this case your family – will be more willing to involve you in their daily lives. Suddenly you are an important player in the home field, because you take responsibility for the overall energy at home and contribute to how your partner and children feel.

If your partner or children are too much to handle or don't feel good, then try to figure out if you have influenced them yourself, or if they have been influenced by others to behave in the way they do. If the latter is the case, then send back the energy to those who caused the unbalanced energy in your partner and/or children by repeating the following mantra, where you can replace 'X' with the name of your partner or your child(ren):

> *"I now pull all of 'X's rightful energy*
> *back to him/herself from others*
> *– in a cleansed form –*
> *and I send everyone else's energy*
> *out of 'X's energy field and body*
> *and return it in its original form*
> *to where it originally came from."*

It's a very simple Energy Self-Defense tool and it works, especially for children, who are usually very sensitive to positive and balanced energy as well as to imbalanced energies in their surroundings.

You can also help your parents, siblings and other family members, as well as your friends, colleagues and others by using the same mantra, and no one will ever blame you for helping them out on different matters. Obviously, it would be much better if they too learned some Energy Self-Defense tools, so suggest that they read one or more books from this series and see what happens.

When other people challenge you and try to drain your personal energy, take a deep breath and try to stay as grounded as possible, even if they are screaming right in your face. Good grounding is essential if you don't want to lose your balance and temper.

Whenever you need time to yourself to think things over, get some fresh air or go for a walk in nature. You can also bring your partner and children, even if they are the ones you wish to get away from. Have fun together, make a campfire and bring something to eat and drink, so you can all have a "peace drink" or "peace picnic" that will remind you to calm down and share your inner thoughts and worries with each other. When we are out in nature, all people get in better contact with themselves and their inner balance. Not many people argue with each other when being out in nature.

Among other important "energy issues" related to your children's body balance, there are external influences, which you can actually do something about.

Make sure that your children have not eaten too much sugar or consumed soft drinks all day, which contain large amounts of refined and artificial sugar. Refined and artificial sugar in large doses is really bad for the brain balance and speeds up the energy frequency in the body in a very fast and often unbalanced way.

Drinking lots of water can usually help the body to quickly remove the over-excited energy out of the body.

Devices we use on a daily basis can cause energy imbalance, so make sure that your children are not sitting in front of the computer or the television all the time, have the iPad on their lap, or walk around with their cell phone in their pocket all day. This exposes them to radiation which can influence their brain and body balance, as well as their sleep, in a negative way. The same goes for you and your partner.

Everyone should always sleep as far away as you possibly can from your computer, cell phone or other electronic equipment. You will notice that you get a better and more refreshing night's sleep. If you have ever slept outdoors, then you will know that you generally feel much more refreshed in the morning after sleeping outside than if you had slept indoors. This is because spending time outside naturally recharges the body.

Watching a lot of movies, reality shows and documentaries that focus on survival, fighting for success, danger, crime, and daily drama between people is usually not the best thing for young children, as they tend to believe that this is how life is in other families and places around the world. Instead, make sure that a balanced reality and energy find their way into your children's lives, even if reality can sometimes be hard.

Balance in everyday life is essential when you have children – both for them and for you. There are many ways to create peace and harmony at home.

You could consider playing card games or board games with your children, as it will immediately raise the energy level in the whole house. As a fun change of pace, you could consider playing games in every room in the house to raise the energy level. Your children will for sure love this, and you will all laugh a lot because of the somewhat odd surroundings of playing Monopoly or cards in the bathroom or on the kitchen floor for example.

The more you involve your children in raising the energy in the house, the more responsible they will feel for contributing to the overall balance at home, and hopefully also at school. Try it and you will be surprised to see how easy it is for them to understand the energy concept. However, don't put all of the responsibility for raising the energy in the house on your children, since you are the parent and should contribute the most.

How to be successful in your relationship

The presence of love in your relationship is Success Factor No. 1 and can never be beaten by anything else.

Love is an exchange of energy, but love isn't always met in the way it's given. Love is a very deep inner feeling, and when you're in love you just know it and it's impossible for you to explain why you love a certain person. It's an inner condition that makes you want to embrace the person you love, no matter who that person is.

Loving one another can mean you are giving love to others or you are receiving love from others. Mutual love is where the energy goes both ways and creates a mutual love energy field around both you and the person you love, and this is usually very visible to others.

If your love is not reciprocated you will often feel sad. Then it's up to you to decide whether to accept the situation as it is, or to move your focus and withdraw your energy, so you can instead attract another person who will love you in the way that you love her/him. This is the optimal way to be happy again.

If you want to create a loving and cozy atmosphere when being together with your partner, pink love energy is always your friend, unless you are about to break up. However even then, if you send pink love energy towards your partner/ex-partner it will actually help to create a better energy between you.

Don't accept any imbalances or struggle in your relationship without doing something about it. Your relationship should be continuously nurtured and nourished in a proper way, and it's important that you make plans together and have fun when being together. Be each other's best friends by being honest, open-minded and caring towards one another while at the same time keeping the sexual flame alive in the relationship.

Try to involve your partner as much as you can in whatever you are doing, and don't ever take the presence of your partner for granted.

Always respect your partner and children and don't be dominant in a controlling way towards any of them, so that every time you step in the door they start behaving in a different way.

In many societies all over the world new male trends are finding their way into the core of love relationships and other relationships, because being in contact with your inner self, whether you are a man or woman, is becoming more and more essential in life.

Be you! Many people, who play roles instead of being themselves in daily life, often end up becoming seriously ill because their bodies can't handle being something they are not supposed to be. Just look at any bear or tiger in captivity, where they are tied up and put on display so others can touch them and admire their circus skills. These animals seldom shine in the way they would have if they were living out in nature. The same goes for you if you don't live the life you are supposed to.

Follow your heart and do the things that feel right for you and explore life. You will soon find your niche in life and create great relationships at the same time. Know deep down what you really want in life, and you will find the right partner who will support you in being YOU at all times.

Many people around the world, no matter their age, are not aware of what they really want in their relationships. As soon as they get married they fall into a family pattern that can easily be compared to that of their parents or others in the neighborhood. Listen to yourself and find your own way. If you don't know where it will lead you, then take one step at a time and make sure you feel good about every step you take, whether you do it alone or together with your partner. Otherwise, step back and change direction. Nowadays there are so many different ways to be together in a relationship and as a family, that you almost can't do anything wrong.

How to use Energy Self-Defense in your relationship:

Imagine that you send tons of pink love energy to your relationship, and also directly to your partner, and watch and see a positive change in your relationship.

If you want to explore even more energy work for the benefit of your relationship, we warmly recommend that you read the energy guide *"Energy Self-Defense for Love Couples"*. It will provide you with specific love energy tools that can help your relationship get back on track if you encounter any unpredictable bumps in the road.

How to listen to a friend in need

There is no better feeling than to be able to help a good friend by listening to him when he is telling you about his worries – that's what friends are for, right?

Since it's a good friend, whom you perhaps have known for years and trust, you tend to relax more than usual, because it's a 'safe' environment for you. When helping a friend you usually get more involved energy-wise when listening to each other than you would with anyone else. When this happens, you start to mix energy with each other.

When the energy from your friend mixes with your own energy, you will actually start to feel his worry energy in your body and mind as if it was your own energy, which is what you are reacting to.

If you are very conscious about energy and know how to take care of your own energy, you can still also pick up on the other person's worries. This will usually occur because you have experienced the same situation yourself, or because you can easily relate to it.

It could also be that you belong to the unique group of men that are more emotional than the average man, because you have an empathetic, intuitive and adaptive personality. However, most of the time, you can feel your friend's energy within you because it's a trusted friend. Therefore, you will have your guards down, and the two of you will most likely exchange energies.

Now this can be a good thing as mentioned in the 2nd bullet point in the chapter *The 3 ways of exchanging energy*, where the energy is voluntarily going one way. If you have made a conscious decision to help your friend by either supporting him with good advice or helping him with practical issues to make life easier for him, you should still use Energy Self-Defense tools when you leave your friend. This is because the longer your energies are mixed, the more work is required to untangle and clean the energies.

So even if you voluntarily choose to help your friend, you should still take good care of your personal energy. Actually, you should only use your excess energy to help others, but if it's a close friend or your family, you will usually want to help them no matter whether you have the energy or not. As you start to make use of your own energy that should otherwise be used for balancing your body and mind, you will find yourself getting tired and exhausted. So even if you want to help your friend, you cannot allow yourself to use all of your energy on him, because then you risk being low on energy yourself. Especially if you have to go to work and have other responsibilities.

When you leave your friend, you should use the Energy Self-Defense tool where you simply pull back all of your energy and clean it, as well as send your friend's energy back to him in the form that you received it. Instead of giving your friend your energy, you can send him lots of pure love just like you would do with your partner and children, and then he will feel your support (without it being sexual in nature).

Say the sentence on the following page in your head, or picture it taking place.

How to protect
your personal energy

It's important to always be aware of where your personal boundaries are in relation to both your personal energy and to others around you. You might have different boundaries with your partner, children, parents, family members, or your boss, friends, and even your neighbors. Creating and protecting your personal boundaries will help you to avoid losing personal energy.

The most common way to avoid losing personal energy is by making others aware of where your personal boundaries are, and clearly communicating this to them in a respectful way. If this doesn't work or isn't possible, then you can use the Energy Self-Defense tools mentioned in this book to influence the invisible energy around you (also called your radiance or aura), so that others hopefully respond to you in a way that you want.

Say the following sentence in your head or picture it taking place:

"I now pull all my rightful energy
back to myself from 'X'
– in a cleansed form –
and I send the energy of 'X'
out of my own energy field
and return it to him/her."

If you are unable to see in your mind's eye that the sorting and clean-up process is taking place, just repeat the sentence as many times as the situation allows.

If you find it difficult to set boundaries and say no, you might want to make use of the boundary-setting blue color that creates distance between people. You can use the blue color in your clothing, as well as in the thoughts you send out towards the trespassing person. The blue color helps you to say yes or no at the right time.

If other people continuously talk to you, want to debate or argue with you against your will, or are verbally strong, then you can place a thin wall of boundary-setting blue energy between you and the other person. This will cause the person to show you more respect and accept your way of being.

If the person is still not respecting your boundaries and is overruling you completely, you can place a thick wall of blue energy between both of you, which is very effective. Many useless quarrels have petered out in this way, and the Energy Self-Defense recipe you should use is very simple. Just say the following sentence out loud or quietly to yourself, and repeat it as often as you can. You can do this whether or not you're with the difficult person at the moment:

"I now place a thick wall
of blue boundary-setting energy
between me and 'X' to get 'X' to listen to me
and show me respect."

Please note that the blue energy is not to be abused just for the sake of winning an argument.

How to dissolve negative experiences

You know how good it feels when the weight of something very heavy is lifted off of your shoulders. You can sleep better, have more happiness, and live your life in a stress-free way.

Forgiveness is an excellent Energy Self-Defense tool to use in relation to adverse incidents and experiences of an earlier date that you haven't yet cleaned out of your energy system. It also works well in connection with future incidents.

You must forgive the other party for what happened, and yourself for not letting go of the incident, which you might have been carrying around for a long time. Forgiveness dissolves negative energies and bonds between you and others completely, so each of you can make a fresh start. This works even if it is only you who is forgiving and letting go of the past.

For example, perhaps you and your childhood sweetheart broke up in an unfortunate way many years ago, or you haven't seen your best friend since you unknowingly kissed his girlfriend. Once you have practiced forgiveness, then each of you will feel the negative energies and ties between you loosen and dissolve, even if you live in different parts of the world.

To forgive and let go say the following mantra:

*"I now forgive myself and 'X' for what happened,
and I forgive myself
for not previously letting go.
I now let go of all that happened
and create space
for new positive experiences in my life."*

Forgiveness can also dissolve any feeling of guilt or bad conscience towards yourself or others that you have been carrying around. A bad conscience can really drain you of energy, and so can the feeling of fighting with yourself by not giving yourself permission to show your true self to yourself and/or to others.

How to handle hate

As men usually have large amounts of testosterone in their body, it feels much more natural for them to hate others than it does for women. Men usually behave in a more aggressive, fast, and violent way than women, which can easily lead to them hating those they disagree with.

When women act in the same way, they are usually perceived as bitches.

Hate, however, is a "killing machine" that kills you with your own negative thoughts and makes you feel aggressive. Always pay attention to your own thoughts whenever you get so angry that you can't control yourself. It's actually in those moments that you start poisoning yourself with all the negativity that you allow to pass through your brain and body – thoughts that are influenced by you not liking certain people and/or their behavior, actions, mind-set, belief system, personality, etc.

Don't ever invest so much energy into others that you risk hurting yourself because of negativity growing in your mind. It is okay that you disagree with others and that you don't like them, but if you let the hate fester in you, it's like inviting trillions of cancer cells to invade your body. Then the situation will soon get out of control. This is not to say that all people with cancer have it because they have had lots of negative thoughts. There are many different reasons for getting cancer, but allowing other people's life values to invade your energy system in a negative way is for sure one of them.

Instead of internalizing negativity, try to neutralize your own anger by blessing yourself and those you hate, so that your body will not be influenced by either your own negative thoughts, or by other people's energies in a negative way.

You can actually bless and neutralize any negative energy between you and others, so you end up forgiving them and become more tolerant. You can also neutralize any unfortunate events that they have exposed you to, so you simply reset the relationship and/or your feelings about the people who provoke and disturb your inner balance.

Bless yourself and others, and stop hating by saying the following mantra:

"I now forgive myself and 'X'
for what made me angry,
and I forgive myself
because I have kept the anger in me.
I now let go of all that disturbed my inner balance
and create space
for new positive energy in my life."

How to protect
your personal belongings

By using Energy Self-Defense you can protect your things in several different ways, especially if you are a busy person who often lacks time to focus on little details in daily life. Energy Self-Defense is similar to installing an invisible security measure that ensures that people with negative intentions do not come close to the things that you want to protect.

Fear of losing your belongings is often an unconscious and negative energy that can attract persons and situations, and can trigger the unconscious energy that you send out.

Being careful about your belongings confirms that you are a responsible person. However, when being careless for example with your cell phone or your keys, then you are sending out an invisible but clear signal to your surroundings that you don't care so much about these things. This is the case every time you place indifferent energy around your belongings, because then you are more likely to lose them or have them stolen (thieves sense this subconsciously).

To protect an object, you must first embrace it with a divine protective bubble of white light/energy, which makes all negative influences disappear. The object will then be registered only by those who have positive thoughts about it. If an object should be totally invisible to others, a divine thin blue protective and boundary-setting bubble should then be placed around the white bubble.

The color blue in larger amounts is impenetrable. However, use it cautiously, because you run the risk of not being able to find your own things again! You can actually protect your belongings too well so that they will also become invisible to you. So in most cases it is enough to protect your things by using the divine white bubble.

If you go out of town and want to protect your home against burglars, you can embrace the home, the garage, the car, the garden and the swimming pool with a divine white protective bubble, and then place a thin blue divine protective bubble around it.

You can also protect your car when it's parked in a public location. Just don't overdo the size of the boundary-setting blue bubble, because you risk having difficulty finding your car, especially if it's parked in a large parking lot.

You can use one or both of the following mantras to protect your belongings. Just replace 'X' with the item that you want to protect:

"I now embrace 'X'
with a Divine protective bubble of white light/energy,
so it is registered only
by those who have positive thoughts about it."

"I now embrace 'X'
with a Divine thin blue protective
and boundary-setting bubble
that is placed around the white bubble
which makes all negative influences disappear."

How to bless yourself and your personal belongings

Just as we protect an object and send it lots of white light, you can also bless yourself and others in the same way.

You can bless yourself and others, if you or they have done something stupid or something that you feel really bad about. In this way you neutralize the incident and all other past events that have a negative energy around them. This doesn't mean that others will forget what you/they did. Instead the negative energy around the situation(s) will dissolve and be replaced by positive energy, which creates space for an overall understanding and acceptance of what happened.

If you want certain people out of your life for whatever reason, you should bless them in large quantities. Then your relationship or connection can suddenly change in a positive direction and be interesting (again) for both of you, if there has been a lot of negativity going on between you previously.

What most men find very interesting is that you can actually bless your car if it doesn't run properly. The energy around the car will then change in a positive way, creating a good solution where either the car will begin to run properly, be repaired at a fair price, or you may simply find another car that already works perfectly instead.

You can also bless your car if you want to sell it, so that it is surrounded by positive energy. Then you can be sure to receive a fair and honest deal, where both you and the buyer are satisfied with the outcome.

Don't ever send negative thoughts on your belongings, as this will create a lot of bad energy that doesn't benefit you in any way. Instead, surround your belongings with good energy if you want to sell them or give them away, so that others can have a good experience with them.

Whether it's the lawn mower or your motorcycle, bless your belongings as many times as possible to balance out whatever negative energy that you or others have surrounded them with.

Material objects have no soul, but they have an energy pattern corresponding to the energies that those who created them, have put into them. Perhaps it's those energies you are responding to, when you feel that you don't like certain things. However, it is not okay that you have a bad experience with things that you buy, because those who made them had a bad day at work. So always remember to bless the things that you buy, whether you buy them for yourself or others, so they get a positive energy around them from the moment you bring them home.

It's very simple to bless an item, yourself, or others. Just replace 'X' with the item or the name of the person that you want to bless:

"I bless 'X' and surround 'X' with Divine and positive energy."

How to attract everything you want and need

What you want might not always be what is best for you!

Everyone has their own personal energy, which is radiated in their aura around their body, and thus can be perceived by others at both a conscious and subconscious level.

There will always be people who are attracted to your particular energy because they recognize parts or all of themselves in you, or because you remind them of people they know. The attraction can even take place over long distances. This is why most men and women respond only to selected potential partners on dating sites.

Therefore you will probably meet exactly those people who can teach you things in life and/or the skills that you need to develop, or who can help you get in deeper contact with your inner self.

If you want to influence which things you attract in life yourself, you can use visualization and prayer, as they are very strong energy tools in getting what you want.

You can also use these tools if you want to change any type of relationship – including your love relationship, as well as your housing and job situation. You can attract both new relationships and even change the existing ones by visualizing and creating a picture in your mind's eye of your ideal situation. You should then continue to send lots of energy in the form of thoughts and white light/energy on your ideal situation.

It's very important that you create a clear picture in your

mind of what you want, but you should be aware that what you want might not be consistent with the overall plan for your life. One thing is what your ego wants. Another thing is what the spiritual and intuitive part of you, your so-called Higher Self, knows is right for you.

As there is no form or shape in the spiritual world, these two factors don't always materialize in exactly the way that you see in your mind's eye. Perhaps you visualize buying a fancy car that looks like a Lamborghini, but the car you end up getting is a big van with lots of fancy details that are useful when you have a big family.

Timing is everything, and so is realism.

Many people believe that if they have lots of money, they can succeed with anything in life. Loving material possessions and money and having lots of physical possessions are of course okay, as long as you also help others in need, if they haven't intentionally caused their current situation themselves.

It's essential to understand that in spiritual energy there is no such thing as money. Money can be compared to energy. When you earn money, it can be compared to an exchange of energy, where you deliver your work power and get a salary in exchange.

If you keep your money in a safe deposit box, the energy will be stuck with no flow. This is because it can't make any impact on your life if the money is just sitting there, unless you are keeping it for a specific use, like for a rainy day. If you want to earn lots of money, you have to let the money circulate to keep the energy alive, so you can attract more money.

Just because you don't actively use all of the money yourself, others are of course not allowed to steal or use it in order to make energy flow in their own lives. It's always up to you to decide what you will do with your personal energy and your money.

When you have created a clear picture in your mind of what you want, say the following:

> *"I now send pure white light/energy*
> *on my ideal/dream situation*
> *to make it become a reality in my life*
> *very quickly, perfectly and in grace."*

Prayer can be a great tool in the visualization process, as prayer is a simple method to achieve what is your divine right in life. Just don't let your ego influence what you want and how to say the prayer. Additionally, let the prayer be as simple as possible.

Here are two examples where you can replace 'X' with something that is useful to you like lots of money, a car that works well, a wonderful and loving partner, a big house, or anything else that you feel could be helpful in your life:

> *"God is my loyal eternal Divine Source*
> *and 'X' comes to me*
> *very quickly, perfectly and in grace."*

or

> *"I ask for the ideal 'X'*
> *at the ideal time,*
> *and I ask for inducements for*
> *what I can do for that to happen.*
> *Thank you for letting it happen!"*

Always remember to be open to the things/events that happen, even if they don't appear to be going in the right direction. Often we cannot see how it fits into the big picture until later, so be open and patient.

How to surround yourself with good energy

Whether you are passionate about your job or not, or you love your family or think they are a burden, it is important to always surround yourself with good energy. Other people, no matter who they are, will always respond to the good energy and feel inspired whenever they are near you.

When you're happy, your body will also feel happy. If you don't feel happy your body will feel miserable, and then you are more likely to get sick. You may notice that you feel resistance in your body because you either choose, or have to do things that you don't actually like doing. No matter the reason, it is utterly important to protect your own energy, which can be done by saying the following mantra:

*"I pray for protection from the highest Divine Source,
and I now embrace myself in pink love energy
to radiate love all around me,
both on the inside and the outside of my body."*

Maybe you feel it's a little too much to surround yourself with love energy, but that is what your body needs to feel better, so this is actually not done to make other people love you. Instead it's done to make your body feel loved. When saying the mantra you convert resistance within yourself to the benefit of yourself, and the fact that others around you will love to be with you is indeed a good side effect.

Other people will be more kind and supportive simply because they love the energy around you, and that will help create a positive spiral of energy, which will benefit your health condition and make you feel more motivated in daily life.

When surrounding yourself with pink love energy it will also be much easier for you to attract a new job, a new partner, or new friends, because other people will love to have you around.

How to change the energy around you

The most effective energy tool, and the strongest Energy Self-Defense weapon that exists on planet Earth, is to use pink love energy, even if you are a man, as well as pure white light/energy that stands for divine cleansing. Those you send the energy to will then become more cooperative and friendly and maybe even more loving towards you, depending on the type of relationship you have with each other. All negativity will then disappear like snow in the sun.

Children and animals are particularly sensitive to all energy, and respond very quickly to whatever type of energy you surround yourself with.

If you embrace and surround yourself with pink energy, it will be like wrapping yourself in love, and you will actually be more loved and liked by other people. Even your dog will love you more.

You can use one of the following mantras depending on your situation:

- *"I now embrace myself in pink love energy to radiate love all around me."*

- *"I now send pink love energy to 'X' to make him/her become more loving towards me."*

Energy has the same effect whether you send it to others or embrace yourself with it, because as humans we always mirror ourselves in each other. If you only send energy to certain people, it is only those who will respond to the energy; whereas if you embrace yourself with the energy, then everyone around you will react to the energy. Therefore, the last option is usually the best to use, if you want to impact many people at once:

- *"I now embrace myself in a pure white light/energy to dissolve all bad energies around me."*

- *"I now send pure white light/energy to 'X' to make him/her become friendly towards me."*

If you embrace yourself with the white light/energy that cleanses out all kinds of negative energies, then other people won't feel compelled to confront you with things in a negative way. The white light/energy around you will act as a protective layer, corresponding to the energy you are surrounded by when you say the divine protection prayer mentioned in the chapter *What is Energy Self-Defense and how to get started*.

The white light/energy ensures that you won't be affected by any negative vibrations around you, and that all positive energy can easily get to you without problems. It can even transform negative energy into positive energy, so that you are able to be more objective without being highly emotional and/or aggressive.

Whenever you feel the need to re-set your personal energy and cleanse yourself, embrace yourself with white light/energy, so you can be ready and prepared for new challenges and experiences in life.

How to raise the energy in a place

Most people raise their personal energy level when they feel happy. They also raise their energy level when they are together with other people. You can actually raise the energy level in all sorts of places by having a good time there and by lighting candles, as lit candles usually create a comfortable atmosphere.

You can also see in your mind's eye how you raise the energy level in a room with a negative atmosphere by sending white light/energy into the room, or you can send pink love energy, if you prefer that. More on the benefits of using pink love energy later in this book. For the moment, however, you will notice that when using pink love energy, most people will either be more pleasant and friendly towards you, or they will simply leave if the love energy doesn't suit them. A word of advice: always start by cleaning out the bad energy and atmosphere before sending in love. If more people send energy into the room at the same time, the effect is much stronger.

You can rearrange or remove furniture to improve and create a better energy flow in the room. Consider using modern Feng Shui guidelines for decorating the room.

Place flowers, crystals, natural stones or pebbles in various places throughout the room, as all of these can have a cleansing effect and raise the energy level in the room.

Art and design, especially if it's made in light colors and has an aesthetic and beautiful look, can easily raise the energy frequency in a room or place, and so can all sorts of energetic, funny and intelligent types of art and design. If however the art/design has a very heavy, dramatic, dark and violent expression, as you can imagine, this can influence the energy in other ways depending on the intentional energy that the artist has placed in his/her work.

There are many other ways to raise the energy level in a room or place, and one of the most effective ways is to laugh a lot when being in the room/place. The more people that laugh at the same time, the better. Then all heavy and negative energies will be transformed and overridden by positive uplifting energies and good vibrations.

How to create
a quick transformation

Transformation usually takes time; however with the Energy Self-Defense tools you have learned so far it can be achieved much faster. In fact, if you want a quick, powerful transformation in certain areas of your life, you can **send violet transforming energy on the situation**, place or relationship, but **don't** send it directly to yourself or other people or animals. The violet energy represents profound transformation, and it is so fast, powerful and intense that you should be prepared for an immediate effect. The violet transforming energy can easily get out of control, and can turn everything upside down in all areas of your life that need to be changed and/or balanced.

The color violet can cause a total cleansing in your life, such as: things you no longer need all of a sudden break, appointments are cancelled, or there will suddenly be quarrels in your relationship or at work, etc. This will happen to create space for the transformation, and for the new situation that the transformation entails.

If you embrace humans and animals with violet energy, it can cause vomiting, nausea and sickness, so as already mentioned **don't** use the color violet on yourself or others. It's your responsibility if something goes wrong, and the energy always finds its way back to the person who originally sent it out, if the person had negative intentions in sending it.

If you want development and renewal in your relationships, in yourself, and in your partner, it can be good to once in a while send small doses of violet energy on the relationship.

In this case an immediate crisis will usually occur, but things will soon calm down.

Read more

Thank you for reading!

If you want to know more about how to protect and defend your personal energy within different areas of your daily life, please visit our website:

www.energyselfdefense.com

Through our website you can get more information and inspiration on other Energy Self-Defense guides to read, which will provide you with concrete and useful advice on how to get a more balanced life in your love relationship, with your children, at work, etc.

You can also participate in our online courses about Energy Self-Defense.

If you want to know more about the authors, please feel free to visit our websites:

www.sennovpartners.com

www.annisennov.com

www.carstensennov.com

We hope that you are happy with what you have learned, and have started using the Energy Self-Defense tools mentioned in this book. We also hope to have inspired you to participate in our online courses and read more books from the Energy Self-Defense series.

Please tell your family, friends, colleagues and neighbors about our Energy Self-Defense series, so together we can help contribute to making this a better world to live in for all of us.

A good way to spread the word about how to take care of your own energy is by giving *"The Little Energy Guide 1"*, which is a pocket-sized energy guide, to all those who you love and care about. Write a personal message in the front of the book, and they will always remember that it was you who gave them the book.

Finally, you can spread good energy by giving this book a rating and comment on the site where you bought it, as well as at Anni Sennov's author page on **Goodreads.com**.

Warm greetings,

Anni & Carsten Sennov

www.ingramcontent.com/pod-product-compliance
Lightning Source LLC
Chambersburg PA
CBHW061720120626
46550CB00003B/1296